Birth and Early Years of Gandhiji's Life

Mahatma Gandhi is one of the most revered names in Indian history. He was the political and ideological leader of India, also honoured as Father of our nation, he became an international symbol of the free India. He played a very important role in the Indian freedom movement. He is lovingly called as Bapu. His teachings of 'Ahinsa' and 'Satya' (non-violence and truth) changed the complete outlook of the Indian freedom fighters.

Mohan Das Karamchand Gandhi, also known as Mahatma Gandhi, was born on 2nd October 1869 in a Hindu family of Porbandar, Gujarat. His parents were Karamchand Gandhi and Putlibai.

His father, Karamchand Gandhi was a Diwan (Chief Minister) of Porbandar and an honourable and upright man. Gandhiji's mother was a religious and pious woman. Gandhiji gained high moral and social values from his parents. Since childhood, Gandhiji believed strongly in non-violence, truth, purity and very simple lifestyle.

At the age of 13, Gandhiji got married to a girl of the same age named, Kasturba Gandhi. They had four sons. Gandhiji started his education in Porbandar. He further studied in Rajkot and did his matriculation. Then, he joined the University of Bombay in 1887. His family wanted him to become a barrister.

In 1888, he went to London for further studies and completed his law in 1891. He returned to India. For the next two years, he practised law in India.

Gandhiji in South Africa

At the age of 23, Gandhiji left his family once again and came to South Africa as a legal advisor of an Indian businessman. In South Africa, Gandhiji found that there was a strong demarcation between the Black and White communities. The Black community faced a lot of discrimination and were very badly treated. Gandhiji felt very bad about this.

Just after a week of his stay, Gandhiji experienced the humiliation because of discrimination. One day, he had to travel in a train. He had a first-class ticket with him. At the Pietermartizburg station when he entered the first-class compartment and was asked to shift to the third-class compartment. The ticket checker told him that the first-class was reserved for Whites.

On raising objection on this discrimination, Gandhiji was thrown out of the train.

During this journey, he late came to know that discrimination is the common practise there. The Black community and the Indians were called 'coolies'.

After this incident, Gandhiji decided to fight against this injustice. He wrote letters to the higher officials and began a protest against the discrimination in South Africa.

For the next three years, Gandhiji continuously fought for the justice. Soon, he became a well-known activist and a leader of the Indian community.

On 22nd May 1894, Gandhiji established an organisation—Natal Indian Congress (NIC) in South Africa. This organisation looked after the rights of Indians living there. While working for NIC, Gandhiji also faced a lot of opposition from the other communities. He was also attacked several times.

Gandhiji spent twenty years in South Africa. Thereafter, in the year 1915, he returned to India.

Gandhiji in India

Gandhiji's struggles and successes in South Africa were well known in India also. He became a 'National Hero' in the eyes of Indians. Gandhiji wanted to create the same wave of reformation in India. He travelled to all the parts of India to know the real conditions of Indians.

While his travels, Gandhiji used to wear a dhoti and wooden slippers. He renounced all the pleasures and adopted a very simple lifestyle.

He established the 'Sabarmati Ashram' in Ahmedabad, Gujarat. He lived in the ashram with his family and some of his supporters. Everyone loved and supported Gandhiji.

People started believing in his teachings of non-violence and truth. He got the title of 'Mahatma', which meant 'a great soul'.

The Indian Freedom Movement

India was under British rule at that time. A large number of freedom fighters were fighting for the freedom of India. Gandhiji also wanted the freedom of India but he followed a different path. He began a non-violent movement called 'Satyagraha' against the British.

Satyagraha means opposition, but not in an aggressive form. Gandhiji taught people to ask for justice in a silent way. The movement created a strong wave and became a great success.

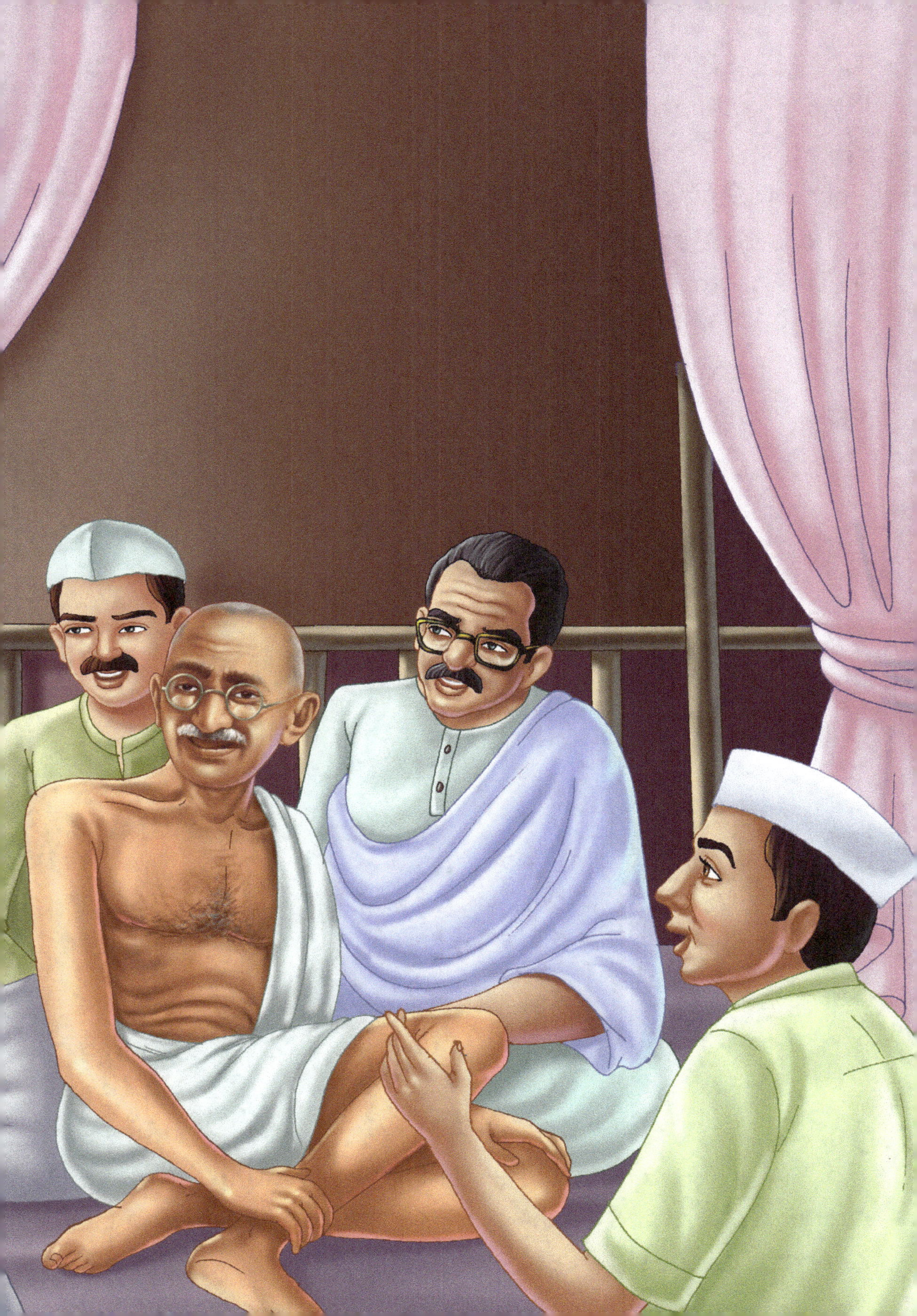

In 1919-20, Gandhiji started another movement called 'Non-cooperative movement'. During his struggle for freedom, Gandhiji was sent to jail many times by the British Govt, but he continued his mission. He asked indians to stop using foreign clothes and other things. He insisted to spin natural cloth on Charkha (spinning wheel). The image of the Charkha later became a symbol of the Indian independence.

On 12th March 1930, Gandhi ji began 'Dandi March' or the 'Salt March' against the salt tax. Gandhi ji with his supporters stand walking 200 miles from Sabarmati Ashram towards the sea.

On April 5, the group reached Dandi, a place along the Coast. Gandhiji demonstrated the method to make salt from the seawater. Soon, the movement spread in the entire nation. Gandhiji was imprisoned once again but, the protest continued nationwide. It was stopped only after the 'Delhi Pact' between the British Government and Gandhiji. The Pact granted the limited salt production and all the protestors were released.

In 1942, Gandhiji issued the last call for independence from British rule. He initiated another movement called 'August Kranti.' Soon after, he began 'Quit India' movement that asked the Britishers to leave India.

After the long struggle and sacrifices, India became independent on 15th August 1947. At the time of freedom, India faced the partition in two parts. After the freedom, Gandhiji tried to maintain peace and unity among the people of different communities.

There was a lot of disturbance in all the parts of country. The communal violence was spreading fast. To stop this violence, Gandhiji began a 'fast unto death' on 13th January 1948 which proved to be a success. On 18th January 1948, he ended his fast only when he got the assurance that the communal violence would be stopped.

Assassination of Gandhiji

Some Indians believed that Gandhiji was responsible for the partition of India. Gandhiji faced a lot of opposition.

On the unfortunate day of 30th January 1948, Gandhiji was going to address a prayer meeting. He was walking along with his two assistants—Abha and Manu. Just when he was stepping towards the stage to address the public, a man named Nathuram Godse fired at Gandhiji.

Gandhiji fell on the ground, saying, "Hey Ram, Hey Ram!" These were the last words of Mahatma Gandhi.

The great soul, the light of the nation, was gone. The whole country was mourning bitterly on their dear Bapu's departure from the world. The other countries were also shocked at his death.

Soon after the assassination of Mahatma Gandhi, Pt. Jawahar Lal Nehru addressed the nation on radio:
"Friends & Comarades, The light has gone out of our lives and there is darkness everywhere. I do not know what to tell you and how to say it. Our beloved leader, Bapu as we called him, the Father of the Nation, is no more.
Perhaps I am wrong to say that. Nevertheless, we will never see him again as we have seen him for these many years. We will not run to him for advice and seek solace from him, and that is a terrible blow, not only to me, but also to millions and millions in this country.
And it is a little difficult to soften the blow by any other advice that I or anyone else can give you.."

India Remembers Mahatma Gandhi

Mahatma Gandhi's Samadhi is at Raj Ghat in Delhi. Thousands of people from all over the country come to Raj Ghat to pay homage to the great man.

2nd October, Gandhiji's birthday is celebrated as 'Gandhi Jayanti'. It is one of the three National festivals of India. People of India still remember their dear 'Bapu' with great love and reverence.

Every year, 30th January—the day of Gandhiji's assassination, is observed as the Martyr's Day to commemorate the struggle of all those who sacrificed their life for the country. Mahatma Gandhi's picture is also printed on the Indian currency notes.

Mahatma Gandhi was a great writer also. He wrote and edited many newspaper articles during his lifetime. He also wrote several books including his autobiography—My Experiments with Truth.

In the year 1930, Time magazine named Mahatma Gandhi as 'The Man of the Year'. There are many books written about him and his teachings. The life of Mahatma Gandhi has been widely portrayed in the Indian literature, theatre and movies.

Mahatma Gandhi dedicated his entire life for the welfare of Indians. He has been the greatest source of inspiration for all the Indians. His teachings of non-violence, peace and truth are still practised and followed by many, not only in India but also in other countries.

The only way to pay tribute to the great man—The Father of Our Nation—is to follow his teachings in our lives. We should learn from the great life of Mahatma Gandhi.

Chanakya—The Pioneer Economist of India

Chanakya is one of the greatest personalities of Indian history. He was the advisor and Prime Minister to the Emperor, Chandragupta Maurya. He was a professor at the University of Takshila and was well known for his expertise in Commerce, Economics and various other subjects.

Chanakya is also known as Kautilya and Vishnugupta Sharma. He was born in 370 BC. He has been honoured by the title of the 'Pioneer Economist of India'. He authored two ancient Indian treatises named 'Arthashastra' and 'Neetishastra'.

With the help of Chandragupta Maurya, Chanakya established the Mauryan Dynasty after defeating the Nanda kings.

Birth and Early Years of Chanakya's Life

Chanakya was born in a Brahmin family in 370 BC, in the city of Patliputra (Patna), Bihar. His father was Acharya Chanak, who being a teacher wanted to provide the best education to Chanakya.

Chanakya received his education at Takshashila (Taxila)—the ancient centre for culture and education. At a very young age, he had memorised the Vedas, which were considered as the toughest scriptures.

Since childhood, Chanakya was inclined towards political study too. His extraordinary wisdom and tact were evident in his nature. His second interest was Economics. He studied and gained expertise in Economics as well.

After completing his education, Chanakya started teaching at Takshashila (Taxila). He believed in sharing education and knowledge with others, so that they could also be benefited by it.

Chanakya proved to be an ideal teacher. He imparted education to his students in a interactive and practical way and hence became a popular and respected teacher of his times. His students came from royal families which enabled Chanakya to know most of the political happenings in the country.

Chanakya once came to know that there were chances of foreign invasion in India. Europe's great warrior Salukes was preparing his armies to attack India. On the other hand, the ruler of Patliputra, Dhanananda was torturing the people of the kingdom. The neighbouring countries were also ready to invade the weak areas of India.

Understanding the internal and the external situation, Chanakya decided to leave the University and do something to save the nation. With this thought in his mind, he left Takshashila and moved to Patliputra.

Chanakya in Patliputra

Patliputra (presently known as Patna) was a prosperous city famous for its rich culture. It was also a business centre. Since most essential commodities were produced in the city. Patliputra always welcomed scholars and artists. Chanakya reached the city and started his first campaign from here. The ruler of Patliputra, Dhananada was a cruel king. Who used to collect heavy taxes from the people of his kingdom, to accumlate wealth.

Chanakya was sad on witnessing the condition at Patliputra. He joined a committee made by the king for charity purposes.

The committee, called Sungha (Trust), was headed by scholars and the influential people of the city. Chanakya was later appointed as the President of the Sungha (Trust).

As the President of the trust, Chanakya used to meet King Dhanananda several times. Unlike other courtiers, Chanakya never tried to flatter the king. He was always very clear and straightforward in his communication with the king.

The king didn't like the rude and harsh behaviour of Chanakya. He removed him from the position of the President without any reason. Chanakya became very angry on this.

The king ordered his soldiers to throw Chanakya out of the palace. While his soldiers were pushing Chanakya out of the court, the knot of his hair got opened. Chanakya felt highly insulted. He vowed not to tie the knot of his hair till he puts one ends to the entire Nanda dynasty.

Chanakya Meets Chandragupta

Walking on the streets of Patliputra angrily, he stumbled upon a stump of grass. He decided to went out his anger in the right way. He sat down and started plucking the strands of grass.

While Chanakya was busy plucking grass, he saw some young boys playing in the ground. One of the boys was acting like a king and others as his courtiers and people. The boys who were acting like the people of kingdom came forward one by one with their problems. And, the boy acting as the king gave solutions to each and every problem.

Chanakya was highly impressed by the intelligence and righteousness of the boy. He approached the boy and asked him, "Who are you?"
"Sir, my name is Chandragupta," replied the young boy. Chandragupta told Chanakya everything about his life and his family background.

He said, "Sir, Nandas killed my father and brothers. Now, I want to take revenge from them."

King Dhananada was also a Nanda king and Chanakya wanted to take a revenge from him. Since, he joined hands with Chandragupta. He vowed to destroy the Nanda king and promised the throne of Patliputra to Chandragupta.

Great Works of Chanakya

While carrying out the responsibilities of the Magadh Empire, Chanakya started penning down his great work. He wrote the treatise on politics and administration—Arthashastra. The book discusses monetary policies, welfare and international strategies and warfare in detail. This book became popular worldwide and was later translated in many Indian and European languages.

Another book written by Chanakya was 'Neetishastra' or 'Chanakya Neeti'. It is the treatise on the ideal way of life. Chanakya also wrote 'Neetisutras' (aphorisms). Out of these 455 sutras, about 216 are on rajneeti (politics) to guide the kings and administrators.

Among his various contributions to the nation, his role in establishing the Mauryan Empire is the most praiseworthy.

Last Years of Chanakya's Life

According to a popular legend, Chanakya started adding poison in the food of King Chandragupta Maurya to make his body immune to the effects of poison. Since during that time it was common practise to kill the kings by giving poision.

Chanakya had no ill intention in giving poison to the king. But one day, by mistake, King's wife-Queen Durdhara who was pregnent, shared the food with the king. When Chanakya came to know about this, he got worried for the baby.

He immediately operated the queen and took the baby out safely. Unfortunately, the queen died because of effects of poison. The prince was named as Bindusara.

When Bindusara entered his youth, Chandragupta Maurya gave the throne to him. He retired from his duties to spend rest of his life in meditation. He went to a place called Shravana Belagola in Karnataka, and lived there till the end of his life.

On the other hand, Chanakya continued to be the Prime Minister and advisor to Bindusara. One of the other ministers of Bindusara named Subandhu didn't like Chanakya. Once, he told Bindusara that Chanakya was responsible for his mother's death. Bindusara believed Subandhu and decided to take revenge.

When Chanakya came to know about the incident, he decided to end his life. He renounced everything, distributed his wealth among the poor and needy, abstained from food and water and sat for deep meditation.

Meanwhile, Bindusara came to know about the complete story of his birth through his nurses. He also came to know that Chanakya was the one who saved his life. He rushed to Chanakya to apologise. But Chanakya didn't change his mind. In 283 BC, at the age of 87, great Chanakya died.

Bindusara repented for his actions badly. He blamed Subandhu for misguiding him. Chanakya's death was the greatest loss not only for Bindusara but also for the entire nation.

Chanakya has been a great inspiration and a role model for many kings and administrators. His knowledge and understanding of the politics and economics was beyond admiration. His theories gave a new shape and system to our nation.

Chanakya's contribution to the Indian history and society as a whole is extraordinary. His life proves that with a strong determination, anyone can achieve anything.

www.ingramcontent.com/pod-product-compliance
Lightning Source LLC
LaVergne TN
LVHW060601200726
843509LV00003B/185